DATE DUE

JUN 2 4 2005	
JAN 2 3 2006	
AUG 0 6 2007	

DEMCO, INC. 38-2931

Germany
the land

Kathryn Lane

A Bobbie Kalman Book

The Lands, Peoples, and Cultures Series

 Crabtree Publishing Company

www.crabtreebooks.com

The Lands, Peoples, and Cultures Series

Created by Bobbie Kalman

Coordinating editor
Ellen Rodger

Project editor
Lisa Gurusinghe

Production Coordinator
Rosie Gowsell

Project development, photo research, and design
First Folio Resource Group, Inc.
  Erinn Banting
  Pauline Beggs
  Tom Dart
  Bruce Krever
  Debbie Smith

Editing
Jessica Rudolph

Separations and film
Embassy Graphics

Printer
Worzalla Publishing Company

Consultants
Sandra Schier, The Goethe Institute; Sonja Schlegel, Consulate General of Germany

Photographs
Archive Photos/Popperfoto: p. 11 (left); Boutin/Photo Researchers: p. 5 (bottom left); Corbis/Archivo Iconografico, S.A.: p. 10 (top); Corbis/Neil Beer: p. 31 (left); Corbis/Bettmann: p. 10 (bottom), p. 22 (both); Corbis/Ric Ergenbright: p. 26 (bottom); Corbis/Owen Franken: p. 17 (top); Corbis/Franz-Marc Frei: p. 15 (top); Corbis/Hulton-Deutsch: p. 23 (top); Corbis/Bob Krist: p. 27 (top); Corbis/James Marshall: p. 20 (bottom); Corbis/Michael Maslan Historic Photographs: p. 14 (left); Corbis/Milepost 92 1/2: p. 21; Corbis/Richard T. Nowitz: p. 12 (top); Corbis/Steve Raymer: p. 9 (bottom); Corbis/Erik Schaffer/Ecoscene: p. 27 (bottom); Corbis/Peter Turnley: p. 11 (right); Corbis/Manfred Vollmer: p. 24 (both); Corbis/Michael S. Yamashita: p. 23 (bottom); Tony Craddock/Science Photo Library/Photo Researchers: p. 4; Aryil A. Daniels, Science Source/Photo Researchers: p. 9 (top); Charle Donnezau, The National Audubon Society Collection/Photo Researchers: p. 30 (left); Chad Ehlers/International Stock: p. 16 (bottom); R. Förster, The National Audubon Society Collection/Photo Researchers: p. 29 (left); Georg Gerster/Photo Researchers: p. 7 (top); Beryl Goldberg: p. 5 (bottom right), p. 12 (bottom), p. 13 (top), p. 15 (bottom), p. 31 (right); A. L. Goldman/ Photo Researchers: p. 14 (right); Karl-Heinz Hänell/Okapia/Photo Researchers: p. 8 (bottom); Holt Studios, The National Audubon Society/Photo Researchers: p. 30 (right); Miwako Ikeda/International Stock: p. 19 (right); Andre Jenny/International Stock: p. 17 (bottom), p. 18 (top); Peter Krinninger/International Stock: p. 13 (bottom); Helen Marcus/Photo Researchers: p. 26 (top); Tom McHugh, The National Audubon Society Collection/Photo Researchers: p. 29 (right); Emil Muench/Photo Researchers: p. 5 (top); David Peevers: cover, title page, p. 3, p. 7 (bottom left, right), p. 8 (top), p. 16 (top), p. 19 (left), p. 20 (top), p. 25; Photo Researchers: p. 18 (bottom); Photo St. Meyers, The National Audubon Society Collection/Photo Researchers: p. 28 (left); Hanz Reinhard, The National Audubon Society Collection/Photo Researchers: p. 28 (right)

Map
Jim Chernishenko

Illustrations
Dianne Eastman: icon
David Wysotski, Allure Illustrations: back cover

Cover: Houses, apartment buildings, and businesses line the Danube River in Regensburg, a city in eastern Germany.

Title page: The Schloss Johannesburg, one of the oldest houses in Germany, overlooks the village of Johannesburg, in western Germany.

Icon: Hops, the dried flowers of the hop plant which are used to make beer, appear at the head of each section.

Back cover: The *Heidschnucken*, a type of sheep found in parts of northern Germany, has long, straggly wool and curled horns.

Note: When using foreign terms, the author has followed the German style of capitalizing all nouns, regardless of where they appear in a sentence.

Published by
Crabtree Publishing Company

PMB 16A,	612 Welland Avenue	73 Lime Walk
350 Fifth Avenue	St. Catharines	Headington
Suite 3308	Ontario, Canada	Oxford OX3 7AD
New York	L2M 5V6	United Kingdom
NY 10118		

Cataloging-in-Publication Data
Lane, Kathryn, 1969–
  Germany. the land / Kathryn Lane.
    p. cm. -- (The lands, peoples, and cultures series)
    ISBN 0-7787-9372-9 (RLB) -- ISBN 0-7787-9740-6 (pbk.)
    1. Germany--Juvenile literature. 2. Germany--Social life and customs--Juvenile literature. [1. Germany.] I. Title. II. Series.
DD17 .L36 2001
943--dc21

00-069353
LC

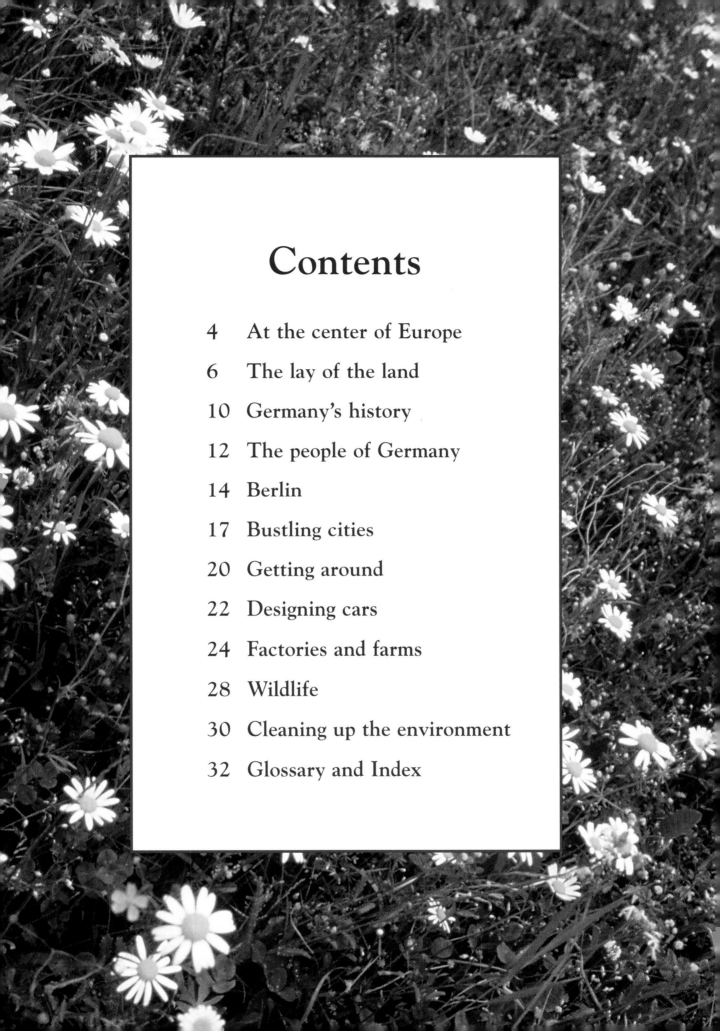

Contents

At the center of Europe

Slow barges pull **cargo** along rivers. Fast cars speed down highways. Cities bustle with activity. Germany is a modern, prosperous country, with busy manufacturing, computer, and banking industries. It is also a country of pretty towns, thick forests, beautiful seashores, and soaring mountains.

Germany is at the center of Europe. It links the eastern and western parts of the continent. Through much of its history, Germany was divided into hundreds of different states. For half of the twentieth century, it was two separate countries. Today, Germany is **united**. Its people are working together to preserve the country's natural beauty and thriving industries.

Facts at a glance

Official name: Federal Republic of Germany (Bundesrepublik Deutschland)

Capital city: Berlin

Population: 82 million

Land area: 137,800 square miles (357,000 square kilometers)

Official language: German

Main religion: Christianity

Currency: the deutschmark and the euro

National holiday: Day of German Unity, October 3

A barge carries cargo along the Rhine River near Koblenz, in western Germany.

Houses sit amidst a forest in the Tauber Valley, in the south.

People visit a busy market in the main square of Stuttgart, a city in southwestern Germany.

An ironworks in Völklingen, a city in the west, is now the site of an industrial museum.

The lay of the land

Germany is a land of rolling hills and wide valleys covered with family farms, small towns, and large cities. Rivers crisscross the country, winding their way past fields and factories. The scenery in the north is very different from the scenery in the south. In the north are the lowlands, where the land is very flat. Heading south towards the highlands, the land gradually increases in **altitude**. Just before the Austrian border, Germany reaches its highest point. At 9,722 feet (2,962 meters), Zugspitze is the country's highest mountain and part of the Alps mountain range.

Along the northern coasts

Germany has two northern coasts, the North Sea to the west and the Baltic Sea to the east. The two coasts are divided by a piece of land that stretches north to Denmark. The North Sea coast is very flat with few trees. Off the coast are islands, some of which are covered in sand dunes. The largest of these islands are East Friesische, North Friesische, and Helgoland.

The Baltic Sea coast has many forested hills and dramatic fjords, which are inlets of water surrounded by steep cliffs.

(opposite page, bottom right) The Triberg waterfall rushes through the Black Forest, in southern Germany.

(opposite page, bottom left) People stroll along the shore of the island of Rügen, off the Baltic Sea coast. Both the Baltic Sea coast and the North Sea coast have many busy ports for shipping as well as beaches where Germans go to relax, swim, and play in the sand.

A village in Lower Saxony, a region on the North German Plain, is surrounded by fields.

On the North German Plain

All of northern Germany sits on the North German Plain. The land is completely flat in some areas and has low, rolling hills in others. In the east, pretty lakes dot the landscape. Throughout much of the North German Plain, the soil is rich and **fertile**, so there are many farms. Other parts of the north are dry and sandy. In the northwest, wide, sweeping **heaths** have rocky soil where little grows.

Across the Central Uplands

The Central Uplands divide northern Germany from southern Germany. The area is made up of plateaus, or elevated areas of land, separated by deep river valleys. Many small mountain ranges, such as the Harz, Taunus, and Erzgebirge, and beautiful forests, such as the Bavarian Forest, are found here.

The Alps tower high above Bavaria, a region in the south of Germany.

Through the South German Hills

Escarpments, or mountainous ridges, run from the southwest to the northeast of the South German Hills, in southern Germany. Between the escarpments are fertile lowlands and lakes. Pear and apple orchards grow on the lower hills. The famous Black Forest, in the southwest, is made up of dark pine trees that grow close together. The trees are such a dark shade of green that the slopes of the forest look black from a distance.

Up to the Alps

In the southeast, the German Alps climb as they approach the mountainous country of Austria. Rock climbers scale the mountain ridges, skiers and snowboarders slide down the slopes, and hikers explore narrow, rocky valleys. The many resorts in the region are popular with tourists, who enjoy visiting beautiful lakes and taking cable cars up the mountains to see the incredible views without making the climb.

The Mosel River is 339 miles (545 kilometers) long. It flows through northern France and western Germany.

Down the mighty rivers

Many long rivers, such as the Rhine, Danube, Elbe, Main, and Weser, flow through Germany. For hundreds of years, the Danube and Rhine have been important transportation links and trade routes to other lands. These two rivers begin in the mountain ranges of the southwest. The Rhine journeys north, ending in the North Sea. The Danube flows through seven other countries before ending at the Black Sea, to the east.

The legend of Lorelei

Between the cities of Bingen and Bonn, the Rhine River narrows as it winds between steep cliffs. This area is known as the Rhine Gorge. One twist in the river was particularly dangerous and many sailors died there. People started to tell a story to explain these deaths and to remind sailors of the gorge's dangers. The legend warned of a beautiful woman named Lorelei, who was said to sit on a large rock at the bend in the river, singing. The sailors, attracted to her singing, would sail too close to the shore, lose control of their boats, and die among the whirlpools and rocks. Upset that her singing killed so many people, Lorelei threw herself into the river and drowned. At the site of the rock where Lorelei sang, there is now a statue and a beautiful **amphitheater**.

Weather conditions

Most of Germany has a moderate climate. It does not get too hot or too cold. Summer days range from hot to comfortable, while during the winter, the weather is cool, damp, and gray. Temperatures are more extreme in the south. There, it can get very hot during the summer, especially when a warm wind, called the *Föhn*, blows. Winters in the south are cold and crisp with piles of snow, perfect for snowball fights, tobogganing, and skiing.

(above) A car drives slowly down a street in Bavaria during a hailstorm.

(below) On hot summer days, people travel to Travermünde, in the north, to wade in the water and relax on the beach.

Around 300 B.C., many groups of people traveled south from the areas that are now Sweden and Denmark to the land that became Germany. Around 9 A.D., these groups fought against soldiers of the Roman Empire, a mighty power from the south that **occupied** parts of the land. Eventually, they pushed the Romans out.

Early empires

One group, called the Franks, gained power over the others during the 400s. By the 700s, the Franks, led by Charlemagne, controlled much of Europe. In the 800s, the Frankish Empire was divided into three kingdoms. The eastern kingdom included the land that is now known as Germany. People of different groups, such as the Bavarians, Saxons, and Swabians, lived there, each in their own area.

From many states to one country

By 962, under Otto the Great, the kingdom had grown to include part of Italy, including Rome. Otto the Great was crowned emperor over what became known as the Holy Roman Empire. The Holy Roman Empire was made up of many small states that often fought among themselves. This fighting went on for hundreds of years. Between the 1600s and 1800s, the state of Prussia, in the northeast, grew in importance. As other states joined it, its power increased. In 1871, all the states agreed to form the German Empire under the leadership of Otto von Bismarck.

Charlemagne made Aachen, a city in what is now western Germany, the center of his kingdom. In this painting from the 1800s, he rules over his court.

In this illustration from 1878, Otto von Bismarck, the founder and first chancellor of Germany, holds a meeting with the first representatives of the united German Empire.

A street in the northern city of Hamburg is covered with rubble after hundreds of buildings were destroyed by bombing during World War II.

The World Wars

Between 1914 and 1945, Germany was involved in two wars. World War I began in 1914 and ended in 1918 with an armistice, an agreement to stop fighting. After World War I, life in Germany was very difficult. Many people were out of work. The cost of the war and the Great Depression, a worldwide **economic** crisis that began in 1929, destroyed Germany's economy. In 1939, Germany entered another war. World War II ended in 1945, when the **Allied forces** of France, Britain, the Soviet Union, and the United States, occupied the country. Germany was left in ruins.

Division

After World War II, Germany was divided by the Allied forces into separate countries, the German Democratic Republic (East Germany) and the Federal Republic of Germany (West Germany). East Germany had a **communist** government. In a communist country, the government owns and manages all farms, banks, factories, and other businesses. The government also sets the prices of goods. West Germany had a free-market economy. People owned their own businesses and set prices that allowed them to compete for customers.

During the late 1950s, West Germany went through a period of great economic growth. Times were more difficult in East Germany. The East German government became alarmed about the number of people leaving the country for jobs in West Germany. In 1961, East Germany closed its borders with West Germany. East Germans were no longer allowed to journey west.

Reunification

In 1990, after a peaceful revolution led by people in East Germany, East and West Germany were reunited. Although East and West Germans celebrated and were hopeful about the future, there have been many problems. The two countries were separated for 40 years. In that time, they became very different places. West Germany was a rich, modern country, while East Germany's industries were out of date. Germans are working hard to help East Germany become modernized, but the cost is enormous.

People celebrate the reunification of Germany in Leipzig, a city in East Germany.

The people of Germany

Over 90 percent of Germany's population is descended from people who moved to the area around 300 B.C. Many other people — over seven million — have come to Germany more recently from countries around the world, including Turkey, Italy, and India.

With over 82 million people, Germany is a crowded place. Most people live in or around the big cities, especially in the Ruhrgebiet, or Ruhr region. The towns and cities in this industrial area along the Rhine River have grown so much that there is no space left between them.

Regional differences

The people who lived on the land for thousands of years, such as the Bavarians, Saxons, and Swabians, each settled in their own regions. They developed their own traditions and ways of life. They wore different styles of clothes, ate different types of food, and spoke different dialects, or versions, of German. Today, the people of Germany still identify more with the region in which they live than with the country as a whole. They keep their traditions of long ago and, although most speak High German, the way they pronounce words, or the dialects they use in coversation, give clues about where they come from.

A man wears a traditional hat at a festival in Bavaria.

Friends study together before an exam outside the Humboldt University in Berlin.

Turks

With over two million people, the Turkish community is the largest non-German community in the country. Most major cities in Germany have Turkish neighborhoods, where grocery stores sell Turkish ingredients and restaurants serve Turkish food. In the 1960s, many Turks moved to West Germany seeking work. They came under a special program that encouraged **immigrants** to move to the country to fill low-paying jobs that West Germans did not fill. The Turkish workers were expected to return home after about five years. Many stayed in Germany, however, and started families. Now, many of the Turks in Germany are young people who have never lived in Turkey. Often, they speak German instead of Turkish.

(right) A man stands outside a shop that sells fruit and vegetables in Frankfurt am Main, in western Germany.

(below) School children gather for a picnic to celebrate the arrival of spring.

Europeans

Many Europeans have moved to Germany as well. Like the Turks, people from Greece, Portugal, and Yugoslavia came in the 1960s looking for work. In 1989, when political changes in Eastern Europe made it easier for people to travel, Eastern Europeans, such as Czechs and Hungarians, began to arrive in Germany looking for work. Other Europeans escaping war or **persecution** for their political beliefs in their **homeland** also came to Germany.

Berlin

The Friedrichstrasse, a busy street in downtown Berlin, bustles with activity in this photograph from the late 1800s.

Berlin is the capital of Germany, with a population of more than three and a half million. The city is known for its exciting nightlife, numerous museums, and huge green parks.

Berlin's rise

At the beginning of the 1100s, Berlin was a small village on the banks of the Spree River. The capital of the state of Prussia, Berlin became more important as the state gained power. By the late 1800s, Berlin was at the center of the **Industrial Revolution**. During this period, the first factories and railroads were built in Europe and North America. Berlin's massive factories produced tools, **textiles**, and heavy machinery such as steam trains. In 1871, Berlin became the capital of the German Empire. Hundreds of thousands of people moved there to find work. Berlin was a crowded and interesting place to live. During the 1920s, it was famous for its lively jazz, theater, and arts scenes, along with its fashionable cafés and bars.

World War II and division

During World War II, Berlin was bombed so heavily that 90 percent of its buildings lay in rubble by the end of the war. When Germany was divided into East Germany and West Germany, Berlin was also divided. East Berlin became the capital of East Germany. Bonn became the capital of West Germany.

The Wall

After division, the West German city of West Berlin found itself surrounded on all sides by a foreign country — East Germany. Since East Germany was suffering great economic hardship, many of its citizens left to find work in West Berlin. In 1961, to prevent more people from leaving the country, the East German government built a wall that was 103 miles (165 kilometers) long and 13 feet (4 meters) high around West Berlin. The Wall was a constant reminder to Berliners that they were not allowed to travel freely. On the East German side, the Wall was guarded carefully by soldiers who were ordered to shoot anyone who got too close.

When the Wall was up, Brandenburg Gate sat on the East German side and Unter den Linden was a dead-end road. Now, traffic flows freely through the arch and down the boulevard.

Oranienburger Strasse is a lively, colorful neighborhood in the former East Berlin.

Tearing down the Wall

Finally, on November 9, 1989, the East German government announced that people were free to travel. Berliners brought hammers and chisels to the Wall and started breaking it down. A joyous party broke out in the streets. Berlin was a single city again! Within a year, East and West Germany were reunified and Berlin once again became the capital of a united Germany.

A changing city

The look of Berlin is changing quickly. Many companies are moving there, especially those that are involved in television and film production, publishing, advertising, and **information technology**. New buildings are being constructed, especially in the center of town. When the Wall came down, most of its route was a series of empty lots. Now, these areas are the sites of huge construction projects.

Potsdamer Platz is Berlin's largest construction site. Many big firms are now building spectacular office complexes there.

Eastern Berlin

During communist rule, many of East Berlin's old buildings were left to crumble or were torn down. Since reunification, old houses have been restored and historical monuments have been repaired, bringing back some of the area's old character. Today, grand museums and embassies, or offices of foreign representatives, line the east's wide avenues. The famous avenue Unter den Linden is bordered with lime trees and leads to Brandenburg Gate, a huge arch built in 1791. Many parts of eastern Berlin, such as Oranienburger Strasse and Prenzlauer Berg, have become trendy areas, full of galleries and cafés.

Western Berlin

Western Berlin is a combination of historic buildings that survived the wars and modern buildings that were constructed more recently. Kurfürstendamm, or Ku'damm as Berliners call it, is a wide, bustling street filled with shops, flashing neon signs, and sidewalk cafés. Kreuzberg is a lively Turkish neighborhood that is popular with students and artists. Its colorful local market, which is set along the banks of a **canal**, sells fresh fruit and Middle Eastern food.

The Tiergarten

The Tiergarten is a sprawling park in the center of the former West Berlin. It is filled with small forests and calm lakes. For much of the eighteenth century, local princes owned the area. They entertained themselves there by hunting foxes. Then in 1791, the Tiergarten was opened to the public as a park.

Much of the park's landscaping was destroyed during World War II. Most of the remaining trees were chopped down and used as firewood to heat people's homes. Since the 1950s, though, the entire 413 acres (167 hectares) have been carefully replanted. Today, the Tiergarten is a favorite place to walk dogs, throw a Frisbee, or just enjoy a break from the busy city.

Germany's parliament has moved from Bonn to the newly restored Reichstag in Berlin.

Only part of the bell tower of the Kaiser Wilhelm Church was left standing after World War II. Rather than rebuild the church, the ruins have been left as a reminder of the terrible bombing of Berlin.

Bustling cities

Germany's large cities are centers of business, **culture**, and industry. During World War II, many were hit by bombs and left in ruins. In some cities, workers reconstructed the damaged areas, which had many centuries-old buildings from long ago. In other cities, the damage was so severe that buildings could not be repaired.

Hamburg

Hamburg is the second largest city in Germany, filled with buildings from the 1800s. Home to many of Germany's publishers and media firms, it is also the country's largest port. Numerous canals and rivers run through the city. They are spanned by 2,195 bridges, which is the largest number of bridges of any city in the world! The Aussenalster, a lake right in the city, is packed with small sailboats in the summer. In the winter, when the lake freezes, skaters spend hours gliding around, stopping occasionally for a cup of hot, spiced wine, called *Glühwein*.

(below) Hamburg is 60 miles (100 kilometers) upstream from the shores of the North Sea, on the banks of the Elbe River. Ocean liners sail up the wide river right into Hamburg, where cranes unload their cargo onto the docks.

(above) Dresden was once considered one of the most beautiful cities in Europe. It suffered terrible bombing during World War II. Since Germany's reunification, many of its ruined buildings have been restored.

Munich

Nine hundred years ago, the duke Henry the Lion built a bridge across the Isar River in southeast Germany. Sailors had to pay at the bridge to continue down the river. A village developed around the bridge's business. It was named München, which means monks or Christian holy men, in honor of the community of monks who lived there. By the 1500s, Munich was the capital of the state of Bavaria and home to the Bavarian royal family. They lived in a grand palace called the Residenz, which is now a museum.

A busy place

Munich has long been the **media** capital of Germany, with its many publishing companies, television and film studios, and computer industries. Today, it faces stiff competition from Berlin.

Munich is popular with tourists because it is close to the Alps, has many museums, and hosts one of the largest festivals in the country, *Oktoberfest*. For two weeks in late September, bands play as people drink huge mugs of beer and eat sausages in enormous tents. Parades and a noisy fun fair with rides and games are also part of the celebrations.

Many of Munich's buildings have been restored to their splendor of the 1600s and 1700s. These more modern buildings, surrounding a busy market, crowd the downtown area of Munich.

In the clock tower of Munich's city hall sits a carillon, which is like a giant music box. A series of bells play a joyful tune, while figurines pop out of the tower to perform a marriage ceremony and a traditional dance. The song and dance end with a rooster figurine making a squeaky cock-a-doodle-doo.

The twin towers of Cologne's cathedral, the Kölner Dom, are visible from almost anywhere in the city.

Cologne

Cologne is a lively city with an area, known as a Fussgänger Zone, whose streets have been completely blocked off from traffic. People stroll leisurely down the middle of these roads, which are lined with shops, market stalls, and cafés.

Cologne developed from a Roman settlement that existed in 40 B.C. An arched tunnel that runs below the streets was once part of the Roman sewer system. The city's most famous landmark is a huge cathedral, Kölner Dom, in the center of town. It took over 600 years to complete! Cologne is also known for eau de Cologne, a perfume that has been made in the city for almost 300 years, and for industries, such as textile production, car manufacturing, and chocolate making.

Frankfurt am Main

Shiny office towers reach for the sky in downtown Frankfurt am Main. This is the economic center of the country, where the German stock exchange and the powerful Deutsches Bundesbank, the German Federal Bank, are located. Frankfurt a.M. holds many trade fairs where businesspeople from around the world sell each other their products. The world's largest book fair takes place in Frankfurt a.M. every October. More than 6,600 exhibitors from over 110 countries display more than 380,000 books. Not all the businesses in Frankfurt a.M. are as huge as the trade fairs. Every Saturday morning along the banks of the Main River, traffic is blocked off and stalls are set up for a lively flea market. Vendors sell everything from clothing to electrical appliances to antiques.

Modern office towers loom high above older houses and buildings in Frankfurt a.M.

Getting around

Germany is an important transportation center. Goods arrive on its docks from all over the globe. Raw materials are transported along its railroad tracks and down its rivers on their way to neighboring countries. Holiday seekers from other lands often take shortcuts through Germany on their way elsewhere, joining the many Germans on the road. To keep all this traffic moving, Germany has developed one of the best transportation systems in the world.

The *Autobahn*

Germany started building its highway network, or *Autobahn*, in the 1930s. It was a way to create jobs for the millions who were out of work at the time. At 6,500 miles (10,500 kilometers), the *Autobahn* is the second-longest highway network in the world.

People who enjoy driving fast love the *Autobahn*. There is no speed limit, although motorists are advised not to go faster than 80 miles (130 kilometers) per hour. Despite being able to drive fast, the traffic does not always move. Over the holidays, everyone seems to be going to the same place at the same time. To help deal with traffic congestion, school holidays occur at different times in different parts of the country, and trucks are not allowed to use the *Autobahn* on weekends.

(right) People get out of their cars to chat and walk around during a traffic jam on the **Autobahn.**

(top) A barge on the Main River carries cargo to Frankfurt am Main.

Sailing along

For hundreds of years, boats have sailed up and down Germany's many rivers. The Rhine River is one of the most important and busiest waterways. In the 1800s, when shipping was the main form of cargo transportation, **engineers** decided that the Rhine would be easier to **navigate** if it were straightened. They undertook a huge project, digging a new riverbed and changing the course of the river. When they were finished, the Rhine was 53 miles (85 kilometers) shorter. Many of the river's original twists and turns had been straightened, but this made the water in the river move much faster than before. The Rhine became more difficult to navigate!

Canals

Germany has many canals. They are constructed to make transportation quicker and easier. The Kiel Canal, in northern Germany, is one of the busiest canals in the world. It links the North Sea with the Baltic Sea, so that boats traveling from one to the other do not have to sail all the way around Denmark.

Traveling in the city

Driving in German cities can be frustrating. Traffic jams the streets, parking spaces are almost impossible to find, and streets change names without warning. In cities, people are encouraged to leave their cars at home and get to work by taking the bus or streetcar. People also take the *S-Bahn*, which is a train that travels from the **suburbs** into the city; or the *U-Bahn*, which is the subway.

A hanging railway

Wuppertal, in the Ruhr region, has a public transportation system that is a little different. The *Schwebebahn* is made up of a suspended track from which rail cars hang. The track is held three stories in the air by 472 massive steel girders. The cars zip along the track high above the busy streets and scenic river.

*Even though the **Schwebebahn** is over 100 years old, it still looks futuristic.*

Designing cars

Germans are famous for their contributions to the car industry. German inventors designed early automobiles and car parts that were the basis of later inventions. Today, Germany is one of the largest producers of cars in the world, along with the United States and Japan.

Gottlieb Daimler

Gottlieb Daimler (1834–1900) was an engineer and an inventor. He designed an engine that he planned to attach to a four-wheeled vehicle. When he attached it to a two-wheeled vehicle as a test, he accidentally invented the motorcycle. Daimler's Einspur, as the model was called, had a top speed of 7.5 miles (12 kilometers) per hour. The body and wheels were made of wood, making for a very bumpy ride! Daimler realized that his engine was successful but that the Einspur was not very practical. It moved too slowly and could not be used to transport passengers or luggage. Daimler went back to designing more practical four-wheeled vehicles.

(below) The seat of Daimler's first motorcycle was so high that the rider's feet could not reach the ground. To help the rider remain upright, two little wheels similar to training wheels had to be attached.

Mercedes Benz

Karl Benz (1844–1929) was working on an engine at the same time as Gottlieb Daimler. In 1885, Benz built the first car in the world. It had three wheels and a top speed of 10 miles (16 kilometers) per hour. Then, Benz started to produce four-wheeled vehicles. With all of the economic problems that followed World War I, the successful company that Benz started was forced to merge with Mercedes, the company that Daimler had created to make cars. The new company became known as Mercedes Benz.

(above) Karl Benz and his daughter Clara ride in the Benz Victoria, the first four-wheeled vehicle, which was built by Benz in 1893.

The mighty Beetle

Ferdinand Porsche (1875–1952) was a well-respected car designer. He wanted to create a small car that most people would be able to afford so that they could drive on the new *Autobahn*. During the 1930s, he designed a rounded car that reminded people of an insect. It was called the Beetle. A company called Volkswagen, which means "people's car," was formed to produce the Beetle.

The Beetle went through many changes over the years, but the original rounded look remained. Volkswagen stopped producing German-made Beetles in 1979, although production continued in other countries. In 1998, the company introduced a new, sleeker design for the Beetle, which is now made in Mexico.

Hundreds of Beetles are assembled at a Volkswagen plant in Germany during the early 1940s.

The Trabbi

The East German Trabant, or Trabbi, sounded like a lawn mower and let out puffs of black smoke. The body of the car was made of a very light material called fiberglass, although some of the models were made of strong cardboard. They did not survive collisions well and were often in bad shape after a heavy rain — especially the cardboard models! Despite all these problems, Trabbis were the most popular cars in East Germany, with a waiting list that sometimes reached twelve years.

After Germany was reunified, Trabant, the company that manufactured Trabbis, had to compete with other car manufacturers. The latest Trabbis were almost exactly the same as the original ones from the 1950s. For a short time, they remained popular, but after a while they could not compete against more modern cars. Trabant was forced to shut down in 1990 after 45 years in operation.

A Trabbi, which is on sale for a very low price, sits on a used car lot in Berlin.

 # Factories and farms

Germany is a huge industrial power. It manufactures household goods, from appliances to stereos, that are sold around the world. The computer industry is also very important to the country's economy.

Iron and coal

In the late 1800s, Germany was one of the leaders of the Industrial Revolution. Natural resources, such as coal and iron ore, were plentiful at the time. The coal was used to supply energy to factories. The iron ore was melted down and processed into iron and steel. The iron and steel were then sent to other factories that produced finished products, such as cars and railway trains.

(right) A factory in the Rhur region, which was shut down in 1992, is now the site of local garden shows.

(top) Iron ore is melted down in gigantic, extremely hot furnaces at a steelworks in Duisburg, a city in eastern Germany.

An industrial region

Many industries were built in the Ruhr region, where both iron ore and coal were found. Raw materials and finished products could then be cheaply transported down the Ruhr River. Much of Germany's coal and iron ore has now been used up. Many of the Ruhr region's factories and mines have been abandoned. The old factories are being demolished and the mines are being filled in. Lush green parks are replacing former industrial lands.

Medicine and microscopes

Today, most of Germany's factories are located along the Rhine River and in coastal cities such as Hamburg and Kiel. They use raw materials that are imported, or bought from other countries, to manufacture finished products. Appliance companies, such as Braun and Bosch, have huge German factories. Medicines are made by pharmaceutical companies such as Bayer. Leica, Zeiss, and other companies make precision instruments, such as cameras and microscopes, which require very exact and careful measurements to work.

Welcome to Germany!

Tourists come to Germany to cruise down the Rhine River, to see castles throughout the land, and to soak up the healing waters of the mountain springs. They enjoy hiking in the national parks and shopping in the cities. Tourism provides many jobs for Germans. Tourists buy German goods, such as carefully carved clocks and fine china called porcelain, made by local craftspeople. In small towns, villagers organize festivals that **re-enact** historical events, which tourists travel to see.

Times of change

When East Germany and West Germany became one country in 1990, the west was a rich, modern place, while the east was poor. In the east, government-owned housing was not well maintained, the streets were full of potholes, and much industry was based on out-of-date technology. Many East German industries closed because they could not compete with those in the west. Suddenly, thousands of East Germans were out of work. Food, rent, and electricity became more expensive, since the government no longer controlled prices. Throughout the country, taxes were raised to try to help the people and the economy of the former East Germany. Now, German companies are opening new factories in the east. The two parts of the country are working together to make their economy a healthy one.

Tourists stop at a market square in Wernigerode, a city in the east.

A man loads grapes into a cart at a vineyard in western Germany.

Crops and livestock

Farms are found throughout Germany. In areas where the soil is not very fertile, such as the northern lowlands and the southern highlands, crops that require fewer **nutrients** are produced. These include rye, oats, potatoes, wheat, barley, and sugar beets. Farmers in the southeast grow hop, a plant whose flowers are an essential ingredient in beer. Vegetables are grown in the southwest and in the areas around Hamburg and Berlin. In the Rhine and Mosel Valleys in the west, vineyards cover the slopes, producing grapes for wine. In the hills of the south, there are cherry and plum orchards, and pigs and chickens are raised for meat. Dairy cows graze in the foothills of the Alps and on small farms throughout Germany.

In southern Germany, cows spend the summer on pastures in the hills. In October, they are brought back to their barns for the winter. The cow-herders make headdresses for the cows to wear while they are being herded down the mountains and through the streets of town. The cow that has produced the most milk wears the most elaborate headdress.

Family farms

In the former West Germany, many farms used to be owned by families. They worked the land full time, planting and harvesting the crops. Today, most family farmers cannot afford to have only one job. During the week, they work on their farms part-time, doing their chores early in the morning before going to full-time jobs and in the evening when they return home. On the weekends, they tend to the farm and sell their produce at markets.

A couple tends to their farm near Fussen, in southern Germany.

Germany's furniture and paper industries rely heavily on timber from the country's forests.

Reorganizing farms

The massive farms of the former East Germany were managed by the government. The people who worked on the farms shared the work and whatever profits were made. Since reunification, these farms have been reorganized. Some farms are now managed by the workers themselves. Others have been sold to private owners. Unproductive farms have closed down.

The European Union

Germany is one of the founding members of a political and economic group called the European Union (EU). As a block of countries, the EU has more say in what is happening in the world than each country would have on its own. The EU also makes it easier for member countries to trade with each other. Normally, when goods are transported across a border, a tariff, or extra payment, is charged. The EU has eliminated tariffs within its countries. EU countries have also adopted a single currency, called the euro, which makes trade even easier. The European Central Bank, which is in charge of the euro, is located in Frankfurt a.M.

Wildlife

Brown bears and wolves once roamed Germany's forests. These animals are no longer found in the country. Over time, the vast forests which they needed to survive became smaller as trees were chopped down and cities built in their place. Now, birds, such as ravens and hawk owls, and animals, such as wild boars and foxes, make their home in nature reserves and national parks. These areas are protected from construction and other activities that might harm the plants and animals that live there.

The remaining forests

Animals, such as squirrels and badgers, live in Germany's remaining forests. The Black Forest, in the southwest corner of the country, is famous all over the world. Waterfalls cut through dark pine trees, and woods open onto flowered meadows where cattle graze. The Black Forest is very popular with tourists, who enjoy hiking on its slopes. Along Germany's southeastern border lies the much quieter Bavarian Forest. The Bavarian Forest spreads from Germany into the neighboring Czech Republic, creating the largest forested area in Central Europe.

The lynx, a large wildcat that was once extinct in Germany, has recently returned to the Bavarian Forest.

Herds of red deer

Red deer live in the Bavarian Forest. They have reddish-brown coats and stand about 4 feet (1.2 meters) high. The males have branched antlers that fall off and grow back each year. The females do not have antlers. Males usually live on their own, while the females live in herds with their young. During the mating season, a male tags along with a group of females. It wards off other males and, if necessary, makes threatening gestures with its antlers. Sometimes, the males fight by crashing their antlers together. A male deer also uses its antlers to mark its territory, by making slash marks in tree bark.

Deer mark their territory by leaving their scent. They have scent glands just below their eyes. When they open the glands, they leave a strong smell behind. Males also open their scent glands when they are angry.

The muddy Watt

The Watt is an area of shallow coastal water that stretches 280 miles (450 kilometers) along the North Sea coast, from the Netherlands through Germany and into Denmark. When the tide is low, the mud left behind reaches 6 miles (10 kilometers) up to the shore. The Watt is the largest protected area in Germany. Half the area is so carefully protected that no visitors are allowed to enter.

Trapped at low tide

Countless small sea creatures and piles of bladder wrack, a type of seaweed, are left on the Watt's mud at low tide. The creatures have ways of surviving low tide, a dangerous time because they can dry out and die or be eaten by **predators**. Mussels, which have a soft body held within two shells, close their shells tightly to keep moisture inside and to protect themselves. Marine worms burrow into the mud to stay wet and hide from predators. Shrimp swim through narrow streams of water to find deeper and safer pools where they stay until the tide returns.

An easy meal

At low tide, the Watt is covered with birds, such as oyster catchers and barnacle geese, in search of a meal. With so many stranded creatures, there is a lot for them to eat. Crabs also scurry about the mud flats at low tide, enjoying a good meal of **algae**, smaller crabs, and anything else they can catch before the tide returns. They have to be careful, because they may become part of the birds' dinner!

Female **Heidschnucken** *have short horns. The males have large horns that curl close to their faces.*

Lüneburg Heath

Lüneburg Heath, in northern Germany, is a quiet, flat area with few trees. The heath is a nature reserve. Animals, such as wild sheep called *Heidschnucken*, are protected there. *Heidschnucken* have short black fur on their faces and legs, and long straggly gray or white wool that hangs from their body. The Lüneburg Heath is also known for a low, bushy plant called purple heather that grows there. Every August, the heath turns bright purple as the heather blooms.

Each year, the heather honey on the Lüneburg Heath attracts 12,000 swarms of bees. Heather honey, which is made by the bees, is a specialty in northern Germany.

Cleaning up the environment

Industry has made Germany a rich country, but it has also had a terrible effect on the environment. The country's many mines, power stations, and factories, as well as **exhaust** from cars, have polluted the rivers and air. Germans are very concerned about the environment. They want to make sure that the nature that remains in their country is protected.

Mining brown coal

During the first half of the 1900s, many of Germany's factories were powered by lignite, which is brown coal. Today, most of the country's brown coal mines have been closed down. Brown coal has harmful effects. When it is mined, the top layer of soil is removed, causing sand and dirt to fly about. The wind carries this dust pollution to nearby cities and villages. It causes breathing problems in some people, and coats everything with a thin layer of grit.

Lignite has made its way into some of Germany's waterways, polluting the rivers and turning them red.

Large sections of trees in the Black Forest have been damaged and weakened by acid rain.

Acid rain

When brown coal is burned, it gives off a gas called sulfur dioxide. The sulfur dioxide mixes with moisture in the air. When rain falls, it is polluted with sulfur dioxide. This polluted rain is called acid rain.

Over half of Germany's trees have been damaged by acid rain and air pollution. Acid rain is also a problem for fish. It pollutes the water, and the plants and microscopic creatures that the fish need to eat die. Even buildings and outdoor sculptures are damaged by acid rain. The acid slowly eats away at brick and stonework, destroying much of the detail that carvers carefully created.

A catastrophic spill

In 1986, a Swiss chemical warehouse on the banks of the Rhine River caught fire. The water from the fire hoses washed 33 tons (30 tonnes) of farming chemicals into the river. The Rhine was so polluted that the water turned red. For 348 miles (560 kilometers) downstream, all river life was killed, including insects, fish, and birds. Clean drinking water had to be brought to many people in Germany and in the Netherlands who depended on the Rhine for their water. The Rhine slowly recovered from this tragedy and governments began to pay more attention to the environmental threats to this river.

Cutting back pollution

To deal with its pollution problems, Germany now has some of the world's strictest laws to help preserve the environment. Owners of factories are heavily fined if they do not cut down on the amount of sulfur dioxide that their factories let into the air. All cars in Germany must have a catalytic converter, a device in the car's exhaust system that reduces pollution. To make sure the environment stays clean, the government carefully monitors the pollution levels in the air and water.

At a recycling plant in Gärtringen, huge containers hold paper, glass, and food waste.

Recycling

As much waste as possible is recycled in Germany. The waste is broken down and then made into new products. For example, used fine paper is processed to make lesser-quality paper such as newsprint. Glass is melted down to make more glass. All this reprocessing means that less garbage goes to the dumps, which are rapidly filling up.

Which container?

The German recycling program takes a lot of organization. Every household has to separate its garbage — sometimes into as many as seven different containers! One container is for food waste such as orange peels and plate scrapings. Another is for glass, which is further separated into clear, green, and brown glass. There are also separate containers for metals and plastics, paper, and anything else left over. Garbage police check the containers to make sure that people have sorted their garbage properly.

Anti-pollution advertisements are found in many cities in Germany.

Glossary

algae An organism that lives in water

Allied forces The group of countries that fought against Germany, Italy, and Japan during World War II

altitude The height of land as measured above sea level

amphitheater An oval or round theater where contests and public performances are held

canal A waterway made by humans that is used for travel and shipping

cargo Goods that are transported by ship, plane, or truck

communist A type of government that owns and controls a country's natural resources, businesses, and industries

culture The customs, beliefs, and arts of a distinct group of people

economic Involving a country's businesses, industry, and money

engineer A person who uses science to design and build structures and machines

exhaust The gases released from a car

fertile Capable of producing abundant crops or vegetation

heath A flat area covered with short bushes

homeland An area that is identified with a particular group of people

immigrant A person who settles in another country

Industrial Revolution The shift from an agricultural society to one that produced goods in factories

information technology The industry dedicated to the creation and distribution of information

media Communication industries, such as television, newspapers, and radio

navigate To steer

nutrient A substance that a living thing needs in order to grow

occupy To invade and control a country, as by a foreign army

persecution The harming of another person for religious, racial, or political reasons

predator An animal that preys on other animals for survival

re-enact Recreation of a historial event

suburb A residential area outside a city

textile A fabric or cloth

united Joined together

Index

1 2 3 4 5 6 7 8 9 0   Printed in the USA   0 9 8 7 6 5 4 3 2 1